to Saturn

to Saturn

Sydney Elise

to Saturn

Published by Necto Publishing
https://www.nectopublishing.com/

Hardcover ISBN: 978-0-9995458-3-6

Library of Congress Number: 2021914912

Editing and Notes by Alison Casper
Cover and Graphic Design by Ally Ciano
Thank you Jodi-Tatiana Charles and Sara Colum.

This book is dedicated to:

Mr. Nazzaro
and
Nicole Bagley

to Saturn

A Series of Pink:

In every year I look back on,
no matter where I am or
where you are,
I find you smiling,
running up to me
with the warmest and biggest hugs;
and you will always be
my favorite childhood memory.

                                No matter where I turn,
                        no matter what splits us apart
                              even for a small time,
                        I look towards you in the dark
                           and you are always there.
                                Thank you, angel.

I spent hours of the night wondering
where and how
I went wrong.
I cried in your arms countless times,
and yet I look at you now
as if you are a stranger
who I wish I told nothing -
it cuts my soul
and splits it into pieces
because I know I did not tell you everything.

                             The most impactful three
                         I may ever meet in my life,
                     and I have healed beyond words,
                                    as two of you know.
                         And if time and distance
                                 splits us apart,
                                   if I split us apart,
                     I want this to be left with you:
                                      I miss you
                         and you will always have a
                         special place in my heart.

1

Fade Into You

A walk home.
Ceased church hours,
and a seven minute stroll
to a childhood home
with the warmth of a childhood friend.

We stood there at the T-intersection,
and I kept the promise I made:
you never saw me cry like that again.

A river of tears you never saw,
but you knew. I know you knew.
For certain I do; and
as I reached the
end of a journey, I saw you waiting
to remind me that in my
childhood memories,
I will always fade into you.

Come Home Please.

I needed a friend.
I grasped onto
the act you called
friendship.

The steps we took -
it took years to get
to where we landed;
apart.

The moments that
connected us could
fill one hundred
scrapbooks.

Then suddenly
the pictures started
fading. You became
jaded.

I apologized for
the pain you had
for reasons I did not
cause.

The apologies that
escaped my mouth
only dragged me under
deeper.

You started new
scrapbooks, and I
congratulated
you.

I forgot about
my own books.
And I kept
apologizing.

Four footprints
became two.
I waited for you to
return.

I search for
you. I still have
apologies to
give.

Write back soon.

Since We Were Five

I see you.
Day after day,
hour after hour,
minute after minute,
count the never ending seconds.

My life is a song and you
have been the bass
this whole time.
But the bass gets softer.
By the hour,
by the minute,
count it by the second.

I see that,
you know.
When you walk,
you slouch, like your back
is pressed with boulders.
Your voice,
it is reaching out
but your words hold it back.
          Why are you scared?
You sit down
like you are sitting on pins -
carefully -
and you you still get pricked.
But you are used to losing
blood.
By the hour,
by the minute,
count it by the second.

Your strides are not powerful.
Unless you are being summoned.
Summoned by a satanic ritual;
a continuous cycle;
a deadly affair.
Summoned by the
hour;
minute;
count it by the second.

Young hearts,
young minds,
young eyes,
and yet everything appears old.
Two lights flicker
on and off
by the hour;
minute;
count it by the second.
I drop to my knees.
You can be seconds away
but it feels like minutes;
it feels like hours;
it feels like days;
skip months, it feels like years.

You are years away.
Your person -
Who are you?
Are you so obsessed with the
        light
that you do not notice when yours
        flickers?

You are right there.
I am counting the seconds.
The more I count
the further you go.
Where are you?
What is even yours anymore?
Are you lost inside yourself?

Are you even in there anymore?

You claim you are there.
You claim you are happy.
Is that true?
The cycle;
the ritual.
By the hour;
minute;
count it by the seconds.
You are drained now.
Deteriorated to nothingness.

A body
without a soul.
Yet you still have not
noticed.
But I have.
I have been noticing,
seeing,
feeling,
hurting.

The Happy Box

Heavy footsteps,
so sad.
They are yours.
Listen how sad
so heavy.
Strained a voice is,
so raw.
It is yours.
Listen how raw
so strained.

Thoughts floating
around in your mind.
They tear you apart,
don't they?
I cannot listen to those;
They are guarded by you.
You never let them free,
those thoughts.

I can see them,
though.
I do not need to hear them.
Those thoughts are so
heavy,
aren't they?
Keeping you down,
they are written straight
across your face,
they are striking
in your eyes.
They tear you apart,
don't they?

I remember the light steps,
you bouncing on clouds.
I remember the relaxed voice,
expressing radiant thoughts.
Did you notice when that
changed?
I did.
I remember the
simplicity of your strides.
Do you remember?

I don't believe you can.

You think there is no
difference,
Yet it is so
glaringly obvious.
You chose the worst,
changed your entire life,
you cannot remember
the peace that encapsulated
your being.
Reversing the worst is
turning to the better,
can you not see that?
I don't believe you can.
You have taught youtself
to hate change
now that you cannot imagine
a peaceful life.

She changed you.
You loved that change.
Now you hate change.
You hate the idea
of leaving Satan.
Stuck in a box,
you have the key.
Use it, why won't you?
Ah but no! *Change.*
So go encase yourself
in a clear box
where we can all see
the horror you wear so
effortlessly.
Praise Satan, your
personal creation of Satan
she is to you.
Wait until your heart is
ripped out, torn to shreds.
But hasn't it already?

Your Privilege

Sitting, waiting
at your feet
for your words -
your scripture;
your platform is
unmatched.
Speaking the words
of your thoughts
and your thoughts only,
your followers
ancticipate;
they crave the words
of you,
and of only you.

I am standing on
my platform,
writing the words
you never gave me the
opportunity to speak about.
And yet,
the eyes will only follow
and the ears will only open
to you.
And to you only.

You say:
"She'll write a poem about you".

Yeah, I fucking did.

2

You Are The Reason

I told you about
all of the reasons.
Thank you for listening.

And thank you for taking
care of yourself
and taking care of me
at the same time.

And thank you for being
the reason why I laughed
and why I am able to write
this poem.

And thank you for having
the strength to keep going
and still push me along
all the same.

And thank you for
simply being.

Thank You, Angel

You remember so much,
and I will remember that
for you.
It is scary -
frightening -
because I cannot erase those memories
yet I feel safe in your lock box and key.
Warmth of the red blanket, I am covered in your embrace.
You do not forget me,
and I will remember that
for you.

Self Illumination

It is in the darkest times where you come to realize
how beautiful your soul is; and
how worthy you are; and
how endless the gifts you have to offer this world are.

(MM/DD/YY)

Words flow out of my mouth
and steal the air I so
desperately need
to survive.
The thoughts I
buried within the
depths of my soul,
pour out of me as if
they are no longer mine
to control.

I fill my stomach with memories
because my mind cannot deal;
but my stomach cannot
keep them down; and
my heart beats to the sound of
nothing.

Survivng as I function,
that is
sufficient;
I exist;
time moves slowly.

By and by, words flow and
turned into stories of relief.
My words flow like a
waterfall as I take in
air so that everything
flows effortlessly.
My thoughts are raw and true.

My stomach is full
with the food I have
learned to trust because my
stomach is not meant to hold
memories. My stomach
trusts itself;
my heart knows its purpose as it
thumps with blood my body can hold;
and my heart holds onto what is
dear to me.

Relearning my purpose,
rewiring my body's functions,
I - too - relearned.
I have to learn.

I learned how to
live;
I am alive;
time is nonexistent.

Goodness

Floating in space,
my mind is airy and light.
Stars circle here and there,
and peace settles in my
thoughts.

Better

Why am I
dreaming about
you?

I keep
dreaming about
you.

I Miss U

It is the middle
of summer, and
I am thinking of
you.

It is the middle
of summer, and
I am thinking of
us.

It is the middle
of summer, and
I am thinking of
how we have not
spoken since
May, or
April, or
Janauary.

It is the middle
of summer, and
I am thinking of
my love for
people - well
my love for
you.

It is the middle
of summer, and
I am thinking of
how will our
paths intertwine
again.

It is the middle   It is the middle
of summer, and   of summer, and
I am thinking of   I am thinking of
our past,   how I am lonely,
our friendship.   deprived of
                                    you.

"You're holding onto a friendship that doesn't exist anymore"

Noticeable are the small
mistakes I made (like the times
                          I decided
                          I was too attached
                          to you),

and
I overlook how
distant you are
because I will always
choose you (because even after
                        all those times,
                        I was still attached
                        to you).

I asked you to care
about how much I care,
and yet the wall between us remains.
You refuse to see through
glass.

So for once, I will say
I am tired.

Freedom

I thought about you
again.
And again.
And again.

The times, promises,
laughs, and care
enveloping what we called
friendship,
and I thought about you
again.

A whirlwind of memories
I desperately want back.

Time stopped as I anticipated a response;
promises we both broke;
laughs turned to tears;
care you no longer have.
The torture of the mind, and yet
you will always be welcomed back.

Road Trip

Do you remember
New York?

A plan we made when we
foolishly believed the
foundation of our friendship
would never tremble under
the shifts in our priorities.

Look into the
New York sky for me.
Take it all in
and remember it was
our road trip.

Unread Messages

Write me a love letter
for all the times
you never answered.
A collage of your words
and not a single one
will be an
apology.

Goodbye

Maybe another day
we will cross paths again,
but I cannot keep tying strings
when I know the knots will
never be tight enough.

And I know the thought of apology
is nonexistent to you.
Do not humor me with
a gesture you do not mean.

Golden Balloon

You never said sorry.
I waited for sorry.
I waited every second of the night
for an apology I would never receive.

From beginning to end
and everything in between,
I waited for sorry as you
floated like the god
you are not.
I laid there with broken limbs,
on the ground splattered.
You never looked down.

A golden balloon
held you high and
mighty like the god
you are not.
I see that now.

I now wait for the balloon
to lose its interest in you,
just like you did in apology.

Your Book

I flip to the
next chapter,
and everything reminds me of
rope:
dangling from
the ceiling,
taunting with
its everlasting yet
subtle swing.
I recognize this chapter:
I have read it before.

Eyes piercing the page,
I try to grab the words
and swallow them whole. I cannot
watch you live this chapter,
but the pages flip faster
than I can save you.
The chapter flips back to the
start
and I watch you relive the same
pages
over
and over
and over
and over...

I know this story
all too well,
I have read it
far too many times;
I once begged you to help me
read this chapter in someone
else's book;
I see you took these pages to
call them your own.

Why did you do that?
            Why did you take
            these pages for
            yourself?
Why am I reading this story in
your book?
            Why can't I help you?
Why won't you let me help you?
            Why can't I rip these
            pages from the
            binding?
Why are you holding onto them so
dearly?

My heart is sinking
into the pages I have read
so many times before;
but they hurt me more
knowing I am reading from
your book.
Slowly I sink into your pages,
into the rope that dangles from
the ceiling.
It taunts me with
its everlasting yet
subtle swing.
I recognize this rope,
and I recognize this chapter,
and I recognize this hurt;
and my tears stain the pages,
and my heart rips open,
and my soul shatters
as I choke on the words
I begged you to change
as you choke for air.

(ps)eu(do)phoria

That is love?
You love him?
I see you,
I see the way
distractions cause the
depression because those
distractions distract you
                from
him.
How is that love?

Life defined by love:
bullshit.
Life controlled by he:
who he is,
what he is,
where he is,
how he is,
if he is.

Controlling the very best of
                you.
That is love?
Who are you
without him?

Consumed by he, one
external force.
Focused on
who he is,
what he is,
where he is,
how he is,
if he is.
                Lost yourself there.
Who are you?
You are him.

Obsessed with
his safety,
his certainty,
his being.
Lose yourself?
                Yes.

Forced the love onto
all those around you.
                Fake love
creating misery
flowing over into
all those around you.

You let it happen,
controlled by the
external force: he.
Identical in creation
he made you of him,
enjoyed replicating
his being
into you.

Fulfill fake love,
recognize flaw,
take one more step closer
towards recognition:
he ends the day,
            say goodnight;
he ends the life;
            say goodbye;
he ends it all,
            goodbye now;
he ends you so quickly;
snaps your fingers,
            snap his fingers;
he is not happy...
death.

Danger you are unto
yourself. You and your
lover. Pseudo lover indeed.

And he will gladly
tie the rope for you.

Canvas

Watercolor cannot paint over
the acrylic pain you layered
on my canvas,
and you cannot paint over
the person you are when we are
not together.

I know, you know.
I found out for certain
months after the fact,
                    even though my intuition
                    never fails.
The lies you tried to paint
over the truth could not stick,
they washed away and
your underneath left the
most dangerous impression
on my canvas.

Fire Mind

It burned the edges of
my skin, and I still
could not find the courage
to tell you.

I hinted once, and
I knew you did not understand.
That is not your fault:
it is mine.

Racing in my mind,
racing with the blood in my body:
who would be first?
My blood always won,
and my mind suffered under pressure
for not being better.

Churning my insides,
I walked away
so many times -
I hoped you would never notice
but deep down,
I wanted you to, and
I wanted to tell you.

Written in Hell:

My love, so precious;
my heart, so full;
my flames burn for eternity.

My hands yearn for your soft skin;
my eyes yearn to see yours;
my flames burn for eternity.

Flames so hot, but our love
was innocent.
Rotting away, I am for you.
You fly above us all,
my forgiving angel.

Forgive my soul,
it burns for you and for us.
It burns for you to fly.
It burns for you to forgive.
It burns for you to love.

You slept softly.
You now sleep softly for eternity,
I wanted you to.

I burned.
I burn for eternity with scars.
Our love died together.
I died loving you.

Golden

It is
satisfying
to look at you
and not see
a god.

"I'm not responsible for the image of me
you created in your head"

Today, I stared at the
ceiling tiles
and pretended I was
looking up at the stars.
Mesmerized by what I
pictured in my head,
only to snap back into reality.

Cyclical You

Treasuring the stem of a once sweet rose,
red like the blood thorns pricked from my fingers
and I hold you like the petals have not dried to dust;
and I hold you like the blood did not flow out of me;
and I hold onto you so tightly.

Paining,

A presence
taking the heart of
a lamb and cutting it
in half, though
it still lives inside
the lamb's body.

Words v. Actions

Words were never our friend -
miscommunication was our theme -
and I think now I have come to terms
that our actions will
always
mean more
because our words failed us
countless times.

Convenience

Drop me off when you need
space
and time.

I do not need a ride
if you cannot seem to offer me one.
I will stay near, though,
to make sure you are
steering straight,
and staying safe on your journey.

Right next to the car, I am,
because someday you will not need
space
and time
any longer.

I know you so well,
I know there will be a day
I get back into that car
and I hope you realize then
that maybe you did not need
space
and time -
just me.

Coffee Shop

The suffocating silence
consumes me as we sit
in an everlasting conclave.
Revive me from the death
of what used to be us
as we sit and stare
in our blind ways.

Soon silence turns cold
and I can only remember
the warmth of the fire
that eventually turned to ashes.
Memories of us turn cold
and I associate silence with you.

Come Back

Left me sitting, and I sit
as time passes by,
the prolonged minutes,
and the endless days.
The promise I leave with you is that
I will wait.

I will stare into the
distance,
where you left me waiting
and I promise I will
wait.
And I promise I will
remember
exactly where you left me,
the exact words you left me with,
and the exact moment you left with
me.

I cannot make promises
except for those.
And I cannot stand
thoughts of me
without you.

Why

My heart feels empty,
you filled it so well
and I miss you so badly
and so does my heart.
Of utmost importance you are
to my heart.

I choke on the words I wanted
to tell you.
A laundry list full of
"I miss you"
and I do not think you understand
how badly I do.

I look to you and I am
frustrated, and frightened:
I will never not trust you, and
I will always choose you.

Chains

Latch onto my
heart,
room only for
one more -
you better be
worth it (please be worth it).

Clasp onto my
heart, it will not break
and you will stay there
forever
as my heart sinks
deeper and deeper.

I cannot find my
whole-hearted love.
Was it worth it?

I Miss U (pt.2)

My heart beats
with hollow drums
and it bleeds constantly.

Love my heart
my hollow drums
desperate for your love
to fill a lonely space.

Love my heart
my open wounds
desperate for your love
to heal a bruising bleed.

"Are We Good?"

I am substituting
irrational and unfulfilling
replacements
for the loneliness
I feel when deprived
of you.

[Heart]

I think
I will continue
missing you
forever.

Gullible

The emptiness consumes me,
I stare into
nothing. The substance of
you, and the smile I
cannot withdraw.
Take advantage of this
moment - of me right now;
where "get better stupid"
is my fairytale ending
you planted in my head,
and I will always see you
in silver cars
becase that was the carriage
you picked me up in.

3:44am

Goddammit.
Days distraction,
fulfilling my destiny.
You at 3:44am
not written in the stars,
only in my mind
3:44am
go to sleep.

Longing

It hurts knowing:
I never actually had you.
But it felt - so much! -
like I did.

Grill Marks On Roses

Burned from the inside
I am still gonna love you.

Heart Eyes

I want a pair
of heart-shaped sunglasses
to remind me
that love is everywhere,
even if it looks like hell.

I want a pair
of heart-shaped sunglasses
to remind me
that love is too close for me
to admire.

Empty

Tapping on the trunk
of a willow tree,
showering my life
with thoughts of you.

Loving you was
the most stunning
up close,
and the most painful
from afar.

Stop Time.

Beauty is existing at once,
at the same time.
Coexisting indeed
paired in our existence.
Love me.

Draining it is knowing
of each other.
Indeed coexisting
in our paired existence.
Forget me.

Forget it,
love forgetting me,
love me
please
forget me,
love me,
forget loving me,
forget love,
love me,
forget it.

Cardio

I ran down the street
for you.

Lover Bird Fool

Forgetting the idea of you
          you are not real.
Fell in love with the idea of
          you.

Carrying rose quartz in my
          pocket
A fool indeed.
Fools falling down tumbled
          roads.
                    Lead to nowhere.

Escape the mind –
my mind
you escape escaping –
leave my mind
for goodness sake
I am a fool –
I know.

Idea of you escaping
escape.
Carrying rose quartz in my
          pocket;
a fool,
a fool indeed.

The Sky Looks Like You Today

Peering through the
windshield of my first car,
driving around and I
see the sky.
The beautiful blues - a
deep blue
with clouds looking of
checkerboards -
I looked at the sky
and the sky looked like you.

Astronomically In Love

Under the same moon,
the same stars.
Living through the same
sunsets,
sunrises.

Our universes collide
at the same exact time
for us to coexist.
It is quiet beautiful,
a wondrous feat,
of the way our stars
align.

Poetic, even.

Our worlds are the same.
Entirely different,
but wonderfully
the same.

Do you think of me?
You did once.
Do you still?
Please do.
Look up.
What does the sky
tell you about me?
Does it still remind you
of me?

It is my signature
of loving you
since I cannot
sign my name
on your heart.

Remember that.
Will you?

Galactic Love

Tiny stars, crescent moons
surround me indefinitely.
My tiny universe
enlightened with energy.

Your stars, your moons.
Your universe.

My stars and your stars;
my moons and your moons.
Too bright,
too powerful,
if they were to ever come
together.

Your Sure Thing

You remind me of the stars
so bright and so true,
but I do not get the time
to see you often anymore.
So in those rare moments,
it does not feel real.

I have never met you. Only in
our empty interactions
because the space and time
between us is so jabbing
to the substance we called
friendship.

Yet in those rare moments -
                    yes, the ones that do
                    not feel real -
I see how bright and true
just like I remember you to be,
and just like the stars
I gaze at each night.

You are out of my reach,
far from my hold,
and all I want to do
is have you.
The image of you
engraved in my mind,
it burns bright like the stars
I cannot seem to let you go,
I cannot seem to give up on you,
I cannot seem to stop gazing
at the stars.

I cannot seem to let go
or give up
or stop gazing
for there may be a day where you
change your mind, - where the
stars will watch me back -

and I promised I would wait;
and I promised I would not forget;
and I promised I would remember;
and I promised I would wait;
and I am waiting
                because you were supposed to stay

your presence is truly empty,
and I love the stars.

Strawberry Bees

Warm like the sun,
blue waters glistening,
fresh fruit on a platter.
Love me, why don't you.
Sweet and whole, and
warm like the sun.

But you are not yellow.
You hide behind the moon,
enlighten what I
worship the most.
The color blue - blue, green:
                those colors match
                ever so perfectly. –
but you are a summer
soul of mine.
Love me, why don't you.
Moonlight on the water:
you look so good.

My heart torn -
shattered -
into pieces;
god, you are so good at it.

The devil looks so good.
A beautiful being of nothing
but evil
and you - the devil -
look so good.

And there will never be a day
where I would not want to love you.

*

Moonrise,
sunrise,
I love you.

Soulmates

Meet along a beach wall
where I watched the sun set
ever so beautifully.
A watercolor painting.

Hoped for it all
a hopeful, a naive learned to be
hopeless indeed: you were not mine
to lose.

I guarantee not a day
will pass without my
thoughts lingering
back to you.

Remembering the days,
the nights of nothing
            spectacular
but spectacular I believed it
nonetheless.

Watercolor drips
a night sky revealed,
glimmering stars like fireflies.
August fireflies.

Hopeful learned to be
hopeless.
You were not mine
to lose.

Heart beats
it remembers you so well.
The mind can only push away
so much for so long.

My heart remembers you so well.
My heart wishes I held on
a bit longer
to the love that never was.

Oh god,
I *knew it* too.

I loved you.
I never told you.

You were
never mine
to lose.

August 21st, 2020

Roughly 11:30pm:
a summer night with
my tired eyes
looking up to you
behind the fence,
and your hand resting
on a wooden board:
"Get some rest".
I remember the exact moment
I fell in love.

to Saturn,

My love for you could not be written in fourteen, rhyming and metered lines. I could not cage my love for you. How unjust that would be to the two of us after all this time. Saturn, you love among the stars with the rings of ego circling you with no end in sight. A story in stanzas I have written to you (very particular I was, this book is not for you: it is for me), Saturn: did you notice? Were you listening to your book? Calling out to you, and ending with confession.

Yet this is where the true ending lies: with you. Saturn, you rule change; Saturn, you rule growth; Saturn, you rule mastery; Saturn, you rule progression; (and you rule Saturn). Preach to the skies, but you are already up there. Do so if you must, but it is the responsibility of Saturn to reach his Saturn.

I told you, you live among my stars and I would love to write more letters if I ever fall back into a cycle - a circle - of you. Saturn, look out at the stars, past your rings, because they are beautiful and calling out to you.

I hope the stars still remind you of me, I am not far from your reach even if we are 817,973,037 miles away. And though I presented that spectacularly hopeless word in past tense, I will sign this truly.

                            Love,
                            Venus

Acknowledgements

The author would like to acknowledge:

These are moments and memories from the author's perspective, represented and portrayed as faithfully as possible without intention of breaking anonymity of whom it may or may not concern.

Any and all astrological references are merely for enterainment purposes and should not be used in an informative context.

Jodi-Tatiana Charles, who offered me the opportunity and first step into the world of publishing.

Sara Colum, a mentor in spreading the love and appreciation of poetry to all those around her. Her devotion to poetry is admirable, and I appreciate every minute spent under her guidance.

The Author

to Saturn is Sydney Elise's first published work. Sydney was the valedictorian of her class for four years and the Poet Laureate for two years at Revere High School, MA. Alongside her role as Poet Laureate, she took on the student-leader position of her school's Poetry Out Load Club. She also interned as a writer for her local newspaper, *the Revere Journal*. Outside of writing, she was part of the Nicole Zervas Dance Academy community for 15-years as both a dancer and student-assistant. Sydney is attending the University of Massachusetts Amherst studying English.

www.ingramcontent.com/pod-product-compliance
Lightning Source LLC
Chambersburg PA
CBHW042000090426
42811CB00031B/1966/J